Contents

NEBS
MANAGEMENT
DEVELOPMENT

SUPER SERIES

THIRD EDITION
Managing People

Leading
Your Team

Published for

NEBS Management *by*

Pergamon
Flexible
Learning

Pergamon Flexible Learning
An imprint of Butterworth-Heinemann
Linacre House, Jordan Hill, Oxford OX2 8DP
225 Wildwood Avenue, Woburn, MA 01801-2041
A division of Reed Educational and Professional Publishing Ltd

A member of the Reed Elsevier plc group

OXFORD   AUCKLAND   BOSTON
JOHANNESBURG   MELBOURNE   NEW DELHI

First published 1986
Second edition 1991
Third edition 1997
Reprinted 1999 (twice), 2000

British Library Cataloguing in Publication Data
A catalogue record for this book is available from the British Library

ISBN 0 7506 3311 5

PLANT A TREE

British Trust for Conservation Volunteers

FOR EVERY TITLE THAT WE PUBLISH, BUTTERWORTH-HEINEMANN
WILL PAY FOR BTCV TO PLANT AND CARE FOR A TREE.

NEBS Management Project Manager: Diana Thomas
Author: Joe Johnson
Editor: Fiona Carey
Series Editor: Diana Thomas
Based on previous material by: Joe Johnson
Composition by Genesis Typesetting, Rochester, Kent
Printed and bound in Great Britain

Workbook introduction

Here are the workbook titles in each module which link with *Leading Your Team*, should you wish to extend your study to other Super Series workbooks. There is a brief description of each workbook in the User Guide.

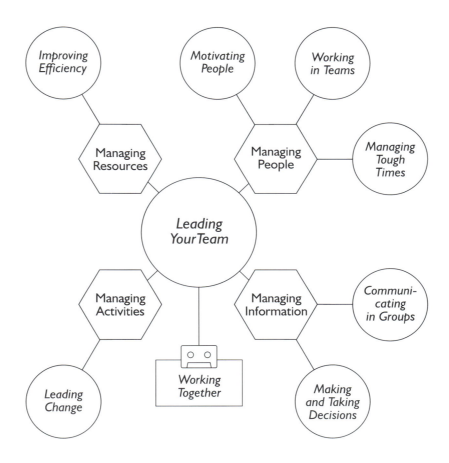

2 S/NVQ links

This workbook relates to the following elements:

C1.1   Develop your own skills to improve your performance
C12.1   Plan the work of teams and individuals
C12.2   Assess the work of teams and individuals
C12.3   Provide feedback to teams and individuals on their work

It will also help you to develop the following Personal Competences:

- building teams;
- managing self.

3 Workbook objectives

A leader is best
When people barely know that he exists.
Not so good when people obey and acclaim him,
Worst when they despise him.
'Fail to honour people,
They fail to honour you';
But of a good leader, who talks little,
When his work is done, his aim fulfilled,
They will all say, 'We did this ourselves'.

Lao-Tzu, Chinese Philosopher, 6th Century BC.[1]

Team leaders are special people. In work organizations, they have the key task of making things happen, not directly, but through the teams they lead. This is a difficult job: one that requires patience, determination, and an ability to motivate.

Many writers and teachers down the centuries have attempted to define the qualities of leadership. Is it something inherent – something you're born with, or can anyone be a leader? And what does a leader have to do? What techniques can be employed, what actions taken, to turn a collection of individuals into a well-ordered, fully functioning unit?

In this workbook we will try to answer these questions. We'll examine ways in which you, as a team leader, can improve your leadership skills, and so help your team to become more effective.

In Session A, we focus on the attributes of leadership itself, and try to decide which of them can be acquired or learned. An interesting aspect of this is a comparison between the skills needed for management and those which a leader should have. Most managers are expected to be leaders, but is a leader necessarily a manager?

[1] Quoted in *Effective Leadership*, page 106 (Extension 1).

Session B is concerned with just two facets of leadership: responsibilities and roles. We will put forward the view that a leader has three kinds of responsibilities, those to the task, to the team and to the individual team member. This three-fold burden, and the leader's many other duties, may result in role conflict or role ambiguity; we look at this subject at the end of the session.

For Session C, the team comes under the spotlight. Every team goes through several stages of growth; the leader has to be able to identify the point of development reached, and to take actions which are appropriate, so that the desired goals are reached.

3.1 Objectives

When you have completed this workbook you will be better able to:

- assess your own leadership qualities and potential;
- enhance your leadership skills;
- recognize the responsibilities of leadership, and the roles to be played by a team leader;
- find ways of developing your team so that it becomes more efficient and effective.

4 Activity planner

The following Activities require some planning so you may want to look at these now.

- Activity 11   Asks you to demonstrate how effectively you assess the performance of your workteam

- Activity 19   Looks at the way you involve the workteam in planning and organizing work

- Activity 25   Asks you to explain your intentions and methods regarding a plan of yours, related to the work of your team

- Activity 28   Is concerned with the feedback that you give your team members.

Portfolio of evidence

Some or all of these Activities may provide the basis of evidence for your S/NVQ portfolio. All portfolio activities and the Work-based assignment are signposted with this icon.

The icon states the elements to which the portfolio activities and Work-based assignment relate.

The Work-based assignment (on page 65) involves gathering views about your leadership qualities and skills from a number of people. It is designed to help you meet element C1.1 of the MCI Management Standards: 'Develop your own skills to improve your performance' and the Personal Competence: 'Managing self – managing personal learning and development'. You may want to prepare for it in advance.

Session A Are you a leader?

1 Introduction

> For leadership is not magnetic personality — that can just as well be demagoguery. It is not 'making friends and influencing people' — that is salesmanship. Leadership is the lifting of a man's vision to higher sights, the raising of a man's performance to a higher standard, the building of a man's personality beyond its normal limitations. Nothing better prepares the ground for such leadership than a spirit of management that confirms in the day-to-day practices of the organization strict principles of conduct and responsibility, high standards of performance, and respect for the individual and his work.'
>
> Peter F. Drucker, *The Practice of Management*[2]

Peter Drucker's words, written in 1955, apply to team leaders in all walks of life, and of course to women as well as men.

Some leaders are tall and muscular; others are small and petite. One leader may be outgoing and jolly, while another always looks serious. All leaders have their own individual personalities, styles and approaches to the task. Identifying the characteristics of leadership is not easy.

But there are many qualities that all leaders have and need. In this session of the workbook we'll be looking at what those qualities are. We'll be asking whether leadership can really be learned. And we'll try to determine what a good leader should be and what a good leader should do.

[2] Peter F. Drucker (1989), *The Practice of Management*, Butterworth-Heinemann, page 157.

2 What is a leader?

An overheard conversation:

'Leaders are born with special qualities. Some people stand out from the crowd. You've either got it or you haven't.'

'Nonsense. Anyone can become a leader. It's a skill and can be learned like any other.'

Activity 1

4 mins

Do you agree with either of these arguments? Give a brief reason for your answer.

_____

_____

_____

EXTENSION 1
John Adair's excellent book *Effective Leadership* is intended to be a self-development manual for leaders and potential leaders.

There are arguments to be made for both sides. Throughout history there have been remarkable leaders, who seem to have had 'charisma' – the ability to inspire followers with devotion and enthusiasm. Some examples that come to mind are listed below, in no particular order.

- Mahatma Gandhi (1869–1948) the Indian nationalist leader, trained as a lawyer and, having spent twenty years in South Africa fighting for better treatment of Indians there, returned to his native country, leading the campaign for home rule.

- Nelson Mandela (born 1918) was also a lawyer, and the son of a tribal chief. He became South Africa's first non-white president, despite having been imprisoned for sabotage and treason from 1964 to 1990.

- Emmeline Pankhurst (1858–1928) the suffragette, was educated in Manchester and Paris and led the movement to win the vote for British women, whose aims were eventually achieved a few weeks before she died.

- Golda Meir (1898–1978) was an Israeli prime minister, and one of the founders of the State of Israel. She was born in Russia (the Ukraine), emigrated to the USA and trained as a teacher, before becoming active in the Zionist movement.

■ George Washington (1732–99), despite having had virtually no formal schooling, became commander-in-chief of the Continental army during the American Revolution, and later the first president of the United States.

■ Sir Winston Churchill (1874–1965) had a privileged background – as the son of a Lord – and was probably the best-loved and most famous British leader this century. In his early life he had trained as a soldier.

Each of these made a significant mark on history. Perhaps you have your own heroes or heroines. (There are other great leaders you might not wish to emulate because they have used their leadership qualities for evil ends – such as Hitler and Stalin, for instance.)

You may agree that most leaders are not born with special qualities, but learn leadership. The leaders of industry and commerce usually fall into this category. Typically, leaders start out in junior positions and learn the skills of leadership as they progress.

In this workbook we are mainly interested in leadership in organizations, where people tend to connect the words 'manager' and 'leader'. But are they the same thing?

2.1 Are leaders managers?

It's part of the job of managers to lead, even though some of them may not seem to do it very well! But does a leader necessarily manage?

To answer this question, we need to consider what the job of a manager consists of. The first difficulty we face is the fact that the role of managers in organizations is changing. Viewed in traditional terms, a manager has to:

■ **plan**

decide what has to be done, and when, where and how it is to be done;

■ **organize and co-ordinate**

harmonize the efforts of the people engaged in the enterprise;

■ **monitor and control**

ensure that what the manager wants to happen really is happening, and do something about it if it isn't;

■ **communicate**

convey information to others, and be receptive to feedback;

3

- **support and motivate**

  others in their efforts;

- **evaluate**

  appraise the performance of others and assess results.

EXTENSION 2
'Traditional manager/employee roles are changing in ... areas like decision making and problem solving where the necessary authority and autonomy has been effectively delegated to teams and individuals, leaving them empowered to think for themselves. To achieve this many managers have had to fundamentally alter their own approach to become less directive, more guiding and more enabling.'

Certainly most leaders at work do all these things, although a leader at the top of an organization may place much more emphasis on planning and evaluating results than, say, organizing and co-ordinating.

Nowadays, however, the work of a manager is just as likely to consist of:

- **coaching** others;
- **empowering** individuals and teams to organize and control their own work;
- **creating an environment** in which employees are encouraged to find out what needs doing, and then get on with it;
- **building trust**;
- **focusing on the customer's needs**;
- **exploring ways to improve performance**;
- **breaking down barriers** to change and growth.

But whichever set of management functions we assume, does this get us any nearer to defining what a leader is? You may know someone who is able to attract a following, even though his or her managing skills may leave much to be desired. And you may know a competent manager who seems unable to inspire others – who has no 'personal magnetism'.

A leader has to have followers, and to get people to follow you, it's necessary to persuade and influence them: to guide their actions and opinions. Some managers are better at this than others.

In summary we can say that the functions of management do not entirely coincide with the qualities required of leadership. As Andrzej Huczynski and David Buchanan say in their book *Organizational Behaviour*:

The functions of leaders are not the same as the functions of management. In some respects they are separate and in others they overlap.

EXTENSION 3
Further details about *Organizational Behaviour* can be found on page 72.

Although managers are usually expected to lead teams, it is possible to carry out many management functions, and yet be a poor leader, because people are reluctant to follow you. At the same time, a team leader need neither have the title of manager nor carry out many of the activities that go with being a manager.

2.2 What qualities does a leader need?

So how can we identify the characteristics of effective leadership? If we think about the enormous range of situations in which leaders are found, it is difficult to see how it is possible to sum up what makes a good leader in a few words. Take these three cases, for example:

■ Frank was a passenger on a ship that hit a freighter and started to sink. Many people on board panicked, but Frank kept calm and helped the crew organize lifeboats. Then he took the lead in getting other passengers to safety. When they all got to dry land, Frank was praised for his presence of mind and leadership qualities.

■ Marek was a team leader of aircraft mechanics in his country's air force. During an emergency operation, it was the job of Marek's team to keep the aircraft flying. This involved long, painstaking work under trying conditions. A single mistake could have caused an aeroplane to crash, which would have jeopardized the whole mission. When the operation was over, Marek's commanding officer congratulated him on his devotion to duty and remarkable leadership.

■ Bettina led a team of computer operators, that had worked away steadily for several years in a large company. The quality of the team's work was consistently high, staff turnover low and the team the envy of many other first line managers. Bettina's leadership qualities were recognized and, when a vacancy arose, she got promoted to departmental manager.

It's easy to spot the **differences** between the three cases.

■ Frank, unlike the other two, wasn't even an appointed leader and yet took charge when an emergency situation arose.
■ Both Marek and Bettina led a team; Marek had to inspire his mechanics to put in a supreme effort during a limited exercise.
■ In Bettina's case, although conditions weren't particularly arduous, she set herself the task of maintaining very high team standards over a long period.

But what about the **similarities**?

Activity 2

3 mins

What characteristics were common to the three leaders above? Jot down **two** or **three** features that apply to all three cases.

_____

_____

_____

_____

_____

You may have noted that all three leaders must have had:

■ **the ability to influence others**

They each had to persuade other people to follow their lead. Tact, diplomacy and other 'people skills' were required. At times this may have meant, especially for Frank, having to be polite yet firm in getting people to do what was wanted.

■ **the ability to inspire confidence**

by setting an example and/or imposing high standards;

■ **managing skills**

> To be a leader, you need more than managing skills.

including the ability to organize and co-ordinate, to communicate well and to support and motivate;

■ **sound personal qualities**

for others to believe in them and want to follow them;

■ **determination**

in abundance.

Judging by our interpretation of these cases, it appears that managing skills are only one aspect of leadership. All the others are just as important.

Activity 3

4 mins

Read the above list again. Are there any other characteristics displayed by effective leaders, that we haven't mentioned? Think of the day-to-day running of a workteam, or think instead of any leader you particularly respect and admire. What other qualities does a **team** look for in a team leader? Try to list **two** points.

_____

_____

_____

You may have included such leadership characteristics as:

■ **dependability**

never letting the team down;

■ **integrity**

being uncompromising in keeping to a set of values;

■ **fairness**

not taking sides, but being even-handed;

■ **being a good listener**

rather than always trying to dominate discussions;

■ **consistency**

not changing values or rules to suit the circumstances;

■ **having a genuine interest in others**

liking people and identifying with them,

■ **showing confidence in the team**

being prepared to hand over power, authority and responsibility to the team;

■ **giving credit where it's due**

rather than claiming all the credit for the leader;

■ **standing by the team when it's in trouble**

and not trying to disclaim responsibility for the problems;

■ **keeping the team informed**

and not hiding behind a 'cloak of mystery'.

Generally, too, good leaders have a **history of success and achievement**.

This is now quite a list. Let's set out these points again, to remind ourselves what we've covered so far.

<table>
<tr>
<td valign="top">

Leaders have:

- **the ability to inspire confidence**
- **managing skills**
- **sound personal qualities**
- **determination**
- **dependability**
- **integrity**
- **a history of success and achievement.**

</td>
<td valign="top">

A good leader will:

- **be fair**
- **be a good listener**
- **be consistent**
- **have a genuine interest in others**
- **show confidence in the team**
- **give credit where it's due**
- **stand by the team when it's in trouble**
- **keep the team informed.**

</td>
</tr>
</table>

Of course, it doesn't mean to say that all leaders are strong in all these areas. History has shown that leaders may have many weaknesses, often including an unwarranted confidence in their own abilities!

In summary, we can separate the skills and qualities of an effective leader into four groups:

- **people skills**
- **personal qualities**
- **managing skills**
- **personal achievements**.

The following diagram illustrates this.

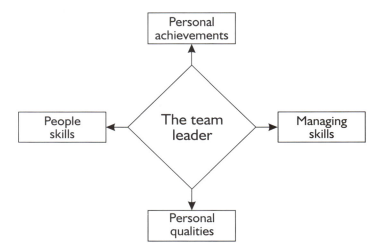

2.3 Can leadership be learned?

Activity 4	5 mins

Categorize the leadership qualities we have listed into the four groups, and then indicate which of them you think can be learned or acquired. (Some of the qualities may well fit into more than one of the four groups.) Tick the relevant boxes.

	People skills	Personal qualities	Managing skills	Personal achievements	Can be learned
The ability to inspire confidence	☐	☐	☐	☐	☐
Determination	☐	☐	☐	☐	☐
Dependability	☐	☐	☐	☐	☐
Integrity	☐	☐	☐	☐	☐
A history of success and achievement	☐	☐	☐	☐	☐
Fairness	☐	☐	☐	☐	☐
Listening skills	☐	☐	☐	☐	☐
Consistency	☐	☐	☐	☐	☐
A genuine interest in others	☐	☐	☐	☐	☐
Displaying confidence in the team	☐	☐	☐	☐	☐
Giving credit where it's due	☐	☐	☐	☐	☐
The willingness to stand by the team	☐	☐	☐	☐	☐
Being good at keeping the team informed	☐	☐	☐	☐	☐

Answers can be found on page 76.

You will notice that in the suggested answer that there's a tick against everything in the 'Can be learned or acquired' column, except for 'determination' and 'a genuine interest in others'.

In a sense, these two qualities are the starting points for leadership. Perhaps you will agree that anyone who doesn't have determination, or who isn't interested in people, may do better to set aside his or her ambitions to become a leader.

Determination is essential, because all leaders have to overcome difficulties and obstacles, as our three case studies illustrated.	It is true that there have been autocratic leaders who have been much more interested in themselves and their own ambitions, than in the people they led. But you have to be a very forceful person to get away with this! Unless you intend becoming a dictator, an interest in people is a prerequisite for leadership.

To be a leader, you need determination to succeed, and to like working with people.

You may have found it surprising that other personal qualities like dependability and integrity can be learned. Perhaps you don't believe it. After all, there are few training schools with 'fairness' or 'consistency' on the curriculum. These kinds of attributes might be considered part of a person's character – you are either dependable or you aren't, for instance.

But there's more to it than this. Often, it is not until people are put into situation where others depend upon them that they display such qualities. And many would argue that these 'personal competences' **can** be learned, or at least developed, although it may take much longer to develop some than others.

Let's review them. First, we should define some of these personal qualities.

Activity 5

Give an example of what you mean when you say someone:

■ is dependable _____

_____

_____

_____

■ has integrity _____

_____

_____

_____

■ is fair _____

_____

_____

_____

■ is consistent _____

_____

_____

_____

See whether you agree with the following.

- **Dependable** people are reliable

They can be confidently trusted to do and say what they say they will. A dependable leader who promises to reward the team will do so. Dependable people are there when you need them.

You could probably think of many examples of people learning to be dependable. Many of us were not very reliable in our youth, because adolescence is a time when people are changing fast; we learn to be dependable as we grow up and take on more responsibilities. Often, people aren't dependable until they are expected to be. For example, new parents learn very quickly that they must always be there for the child: there is no escape from this responsibility. Team members, too, will often appear to be unreliable until the leader puts his or her complete faith in them. You might say that

people tend to be dependable when others expect them to be.

- **Integrity** is honesty and uprightness, or an adherence to moral principles

Leaders who have integrity don't cheat and will stick to their ideals. If there is one quality that a leader gets respected for, this is it.

Although it is perhaps not helpful to talk about 'learning to have integrity', most of us are capable (most of the time!) of behaving with honesty. In fact

to get the respect of a team, you need to be honest with them, and show you care about certain ideals.

- To behave **fairly**, you have to be just and unbiased in your treatment of people

Perceived unfairness is often the cause of discontent in teams.

It is difficult to be fair in all your dealings with others. The main thing is to **want** to be fair – and that doesn't take much learning.

Few of us are always fair. All that others can expect of you is that you try very hard to be fair.

- In one sense, **consistency** is very close to integrity

It also means being steadfast and unchanging: not altering your mind at every new suggestion or setback.

In the managerial sense, being consistent has a great deal to do with decision making. For a person who tends to be undecided between different courses or opinions, it can be hard to learn to be consistent.

11

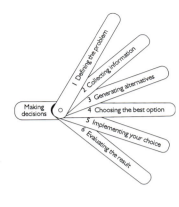

Decision making is a process of:

1 Defining the problem.
2 Collecting information.
3 Generating alternatives.
4 Choosing the best option.
5 Implementing your choice.
6 Evaluating the result.

Inconsistent decision makers may **appear** to waver between steps 4 and 5. **In fact**, what usually happens is that they don't spend enough time and effort on steps 1 and 2.

To be consistent in your decision-making, be clear in your mind about the problem, and then collect facts and opinions before you decide.

So, in summary, we have identified a number of leadership qualities, and shown that these qualities can all – or nearly all – be learned or acquired.

But are there any other attributes that a leader must have?

3 What else does a leader need?

3.1 A desire for the job

Read the following account and then note down what you think about it.

Activity 6

5 mins

■ Milly Covacic was a trained laboratory technician and had been doing the same kind of work for five years, since she left college. She was employed in a large chemical company and Milly was respected by others in the department for her professional skills. She was naturally a quiet person, but she was pleasant enough, and enjoyed her job.

One day the workteam supervisor left and Milly was offered the post. She didn't give it much thought, and, because the money was better, she accepted straight away.

When she started her new job, Milly found it very hard not to carry on working in the same way she had before. She knew it was up to her to lead the rest of the team, but whenever she saw someone doing a job badly she took over the work herself — it was easier than trying to get other members of the team to do it better. When the department manager found out what was going on, she wasn't at all pleased. 'You have to ask yourself whether you really want to be a team leader, Milly, or a technician. If you are in charge, you can't carry on in the same way as before.'

Milly has to ask herself some searching questions. Suggest **two** things she should be deciding in her own mind.

_____

_____

_____

_____

How you respond to this Activity will depend upon what kind person you are. A decision has to be made, nevertheless. Milly must ask herself what she wants.

- Does she really want to be a team leader?
- Has she the necessary ambition and desire, apart from wanting the extra money?
- Does she have the confidence in herself to tackle the job?

If she does, she has to learn to act like a leader. This means a complete rethink of her approach to the job. She might reasonably ask her manager for training and advice.

To lead a team you must have a real commitment to the role, and must have belief in yourself to lead others. This is the most basic qualification for becoming a leader.

To be a leader you have to want to be one and believe in your own ability to be one.

3.2 Do you need to be an expert?

Milly does start with one important advantage, which will help her in her new role. She is a skilled technician, which means she will know the work of the other technicians well. She will be able to help them and guide them, though we would hope not to the extent of taking over their work!

More importantly, she will be able to **spot quickly when things are going wrong**.

She will be respected for her knowledge, which will give her more authority.

To lead others, it helps to be experienced in the work they do.

13

But many leaders find themselves in the position of having less expertise than others in the team; does it matter?

The answer is no, but it does raise problems.

Activity 7

3 mins

What difficulties may be encountered by someone who has to lead a team of specialists, and who therefore has less expertise in certain areas than other members of the team? Try to jot down **two** possible difficulties.

_____

_____

_____

_____

The difficulties may be expressed as questions that the leader might ask, such as:

> 'How can I be sure that what they are telling me is correct?'
> 'How can I assess their performance?'
> 'How can I monitor and understand what is going on?'

or perhaps:

> 'How can I avoid looking foolish and ignorant, faced with all this expert knowledge?'

It's perfectly possible for a 'layperson' to lead a team of specialists: it happens all the time. However, it is important to recognize the possible problems, and to make provisions for dealing with them.

Most difficulties may be overcome once there is trust. A team member who has shown his or her abilities, and is not in the habit of setting out to deceive, can be trusted to impart correct and reliable information. The leader may have to ask that the knowledge be given in a condensed form, using non-technical language. What can be a mistake is for the leader to take no interest in the work of a specialist, for fear of looking foolish. We can't all be experts in everything, but most technical information can be put in a form that the non-expert can understand.

The best and easiest way of assessing performance is by results:

- The software engineer's work will be judged by the users of the programs written.
- The doctor's work is evaluated by his or her record on treating patients.
- Most of all, the work of the team's members is judged by the results achieved by the team.

14

You don't have to know everything your team members do.

To summarize, we can say that, although it **helps** to have as much expertise as your team, it isn't necessary. When leading teams with specialists:

- try to build up trust;
- don't be afraid to question;
- get synopses and explanations in non-expert language;
- judge by results;
- if necessary, cross-check performance and information with other experts.

4 So how do you become an effective leader?

There are many kinds of leader, as the ability to lead has little to do with physical characteristics, educational or family background, or personality. However, what **does** seem to be important is that leaders set their own **standards**.

As we have discussed, most of the attributes of leadership can be learned. With practice and determination, you can even learn to be fair and dependable and consistent. But how? It doesn't seem easy to acquire the qualities of leadership.

Thinking about the famous leaders listed earlier, you may have noted that many were driven by very strong beliefs. Emmeline Pankhurst fervently believed that women should have equal voting rights with men; Gandhi felt compelled to act to defend his fellow Indians against oppression through 'truth and firmness'; Golda Meir was dedicated to Jewish nationalism. We can easily imagine how the behaviour of these leaders would be dictated by their passionate convictions, and that their single-mindedness would draw followers to each cause.

So in great leaders, it seems, standards of behaviour are often the result of devotion to an ideal or belief. For us ordinary mortals, doing ordinary jobs, life isn't usually like that. Nevertheless, in commerce and industry, just as in other fields of human endeavour,

the way that a leader's behaviour is viewed by others will largely determine how successful the leader is.

In many organizations, standards of behaviour are made clear: people know what is expected of them, because there is a corporate 'ethic' which implies a certain code of conduct. To repeat the words of Peter Drucker from our quotation in the introduction to this session:

Nothing better prepares the ground for such leadership than a spirit of management that confirms in the day-to-day practices of the organization strict principles of conduct and responsibility, high standards of performance, and respect for the individual and his work.'

In such a culture, there will typically be many role models for the aspiring leader to follow. The corporate standards reinforce the team leader's message, and provide a strong incentive for the team. The leader still has plenty to do – setting team objectives, communicating, motivating, and so on – but the job is made easier, because team members know the whole company is behind them.

In a poorly run organization, however, the leader who tries to set his or her own high standards may seem to face an uphill struggle. But the job still has to be done.

Whatever kind of organization you work in, you may find the following advice useful.

■ **Find a role model**

if you can – someone you respect highly. Ask yourself what it is you admire about this leader, and aim to reach his or her standards of behaviour. If you can find a mentor – an experienced person to act as your adviser – that would be even better.

■ **Be yourself**

Even if you decide to model yourself on another leader, don't try to copy: do things in your own way, but to the same high standards.

■ **Keep your objectives clearly in mind**

including your personal aims and ambitions. By training your sights on your end-goals, you won't be so easily put off by problems along the way.

■ **Know your strengths and weaknesses**

Remember that few leaders have the ideal qualifications for the job, but the more determined ones win through in spite of their shortcomings.

■ **Stick to your principles**

You will recall the point made earlier: if there is one quality that earns respect, it is integrity.

■ Stephen worked in petrochemical engineering. When first appointed to team leader, Stephen was regarded as something of a joke. He had a speech defect which made him stammer, and was not physically strong. He looked nervous and vulnerable. But, as his team gradually found out, Stephen was wise, open, and above all, steadfast in adversity. He never let his team down, and he always adhered to the principles he believed in, without ever becoming stubborn. Stephen was very able, too, and finished up running the company.

Activity 8

10 mins

Use the following questions as prompts to help you decide the actions you intend to take in order to become a more effective leader.

Who are the leaders you most admire?

_____

_____

_____

_____

What are the qualities you most respect in them?

_____

_____

_____

_____

Who, if anyone, could act as your mentor?

_____

_____

_____

_____

What are your personal objectives, so far as leadership is concerned?

_____

_____

_____

_____

Review the following list of leadership qualities, and say how strong you think you are in each of them, by ticking the appropriate box.

You:	Strong	Fairly strong	Fairly weak	Weak
■ stick to certain principles	☐	☐	☐	☐
■ have clear objectives	☐	☐	☐	☐
■ are consistent	☐	☐	☐	☐
■ have good communication skills	☐	☐	☐	☐
■ try to treat people fairly	☐	☐	☐	☐
■ are dependable	☐	☐	☐	☐
■ like people	☐	☐	☐	☐
■ are always willing to stand by the team	☐	☐	☐	☐
■ are determined to become a more effective leader.	☐	☐	☐	☐

Now explain what action you intend to take to overcome your weaknesses.

_____

_____

_____

_____

_____

You may want to look back at your response to this Activity when you attempt the Work-based assignment on page 65.

Self-assessment 1

10 mins

Complete the following sentences with a suitable word or words chosen from the list below.

1   To be a leader, you need _____ to succeed, and to like working with _____ .

2   People tend to be _____ when others _____ them to be.

3   To get the _____ of a team, you need to be honest with them, and show you care about certain _____ .

4   Few of us are always _____ . All that others can expect of you is that you try very hard to be fair.

5   To be _____ in your decision making, be clear in your mind about the problem, and then collect _____ and _____ before you decide.

6   To _____ others, it helps to be _____ in the work they do.

7   The way that a leader's _____ is viewed by others will largely determine how _____ the leader is.

CONSISTENT	EXPERIENCED	OPINIONS
BEHAVIOUR	FACTS	PEOPLE
DEPENDABLE	FAIR	RESPECT
DETERMINATION	IDEALS	SUCCESSFUL
EXPECT	LEAD	

8   Fill in the blanks in the following diagram, showing the four groups of skills and qualities that an effective leader requires.

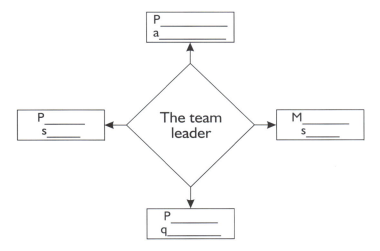

9   Which **six** of the following ten characteristics are recognized as being important in good leadership?

dependability
height
ability to listen
good communication skills
integrity
an extrovert personality
high intelligence
ability to inspire confidence
methodical approach
good managing skills

Answers to these questions can be found on page 73.

5 Summary

■   Leaders are not necessarily managers, although most leaders working for organizations will have managerial skills. The functions of leaders are not the same as the functions of management. In some respects they are separate and in others they overlap.

■   A leader has to have followers, and to get people to follow you, it's necessary to persuade and influence them: to guide their actions and opinions.

■   Leaders have:

   ■ the ability to inspire confidence
   ■ managing skills
   ■ sound personal qualities

- determination
- dependability
- integrity
- a history of success and achievement.

■ A good leader will:

- be fair
- be a good listener
- be consistent
- have a genuine interest in others
- show confidence in the team
- give credit where it's due
- stand by the team when it's in trouble
- keep the team informed.

■ In summary, we can separate the skills and qualities of an effective leader into four groups:

- people skills
- personal qualities
- managing skills
- personal achievements.

■ To be a leader, you need determination to succeed, and to like working with people.

■ People tend to be dependable when others expect them to be.

■ To get the respect of a team, you need to be honest with them, and show you care about certain ideals.

■ Few of us are always fair. All that others can expect of you is that you try very hard to be fair.

■ To be consistent in your decision making, be clear in your mind about the problem, and then collect facts and opinions before you decide.

■ To be a leader you have to want to be one and believe in your own ability to be one.

■ To lead others, it helps to be experienced in the work they do.

■ The way that leaders' behaviour is perceived will largely determine how successful they are.

Session B The team leader — responsibilities and roles

1 Introduction

My own conviction is that every leader should have enough humility to accept, publicly, the responsibility for the mistakes of the subordinates he has himself selected and, like-wise, to give them credit, publicly, for their triumphs. I am aware that some popular theories of leadership hold that the top man must always keep his 'image' bright and shining. I believe, however, that in the long run fairness and honesty, and a generous attitude towards subordinates and associates, pay off.'

Dwight David Eisenhower, Allied Supreme Commander during World War II, and 34th president of the United States.[3]

A lot is expected of a team leader. If you have already led a team you will know that people look to you to be both resourceful and independent. The team demands your loyalty and so does the organization. When things aren't going well, you must still take the responsibility, and when the team succeeds, it is the team members who should get the praise.

But the job has its compensations. Being a team leader is nearly always challenging and often very rewarding. It is seldom boring!

In this session of the workbook we start by looking at responsibilities of the team leader, which can be identified in terms of three points of view: the task, the individual and the team. We then investigate the difficulties and confusion that can result from the various roles played by team leaders and team members, and how to deal with them.

[3] Quoted in *Effective Leadership* (Extension 1).

2 Responsibility 1: the task

EXTENSION 1
The Adair book is listed on page 72.

John Adair, in his book *Effective Leadership*, uses a three-circle model to represent the triple responsibilities of the team and team leader.

Which of these is the most important?

Activity 9

4 mins

Read this account of a supervisor's interview with her line manager, and then say what you think about it.

■ Hannah wasn't happy. She had taken over as supervisor of a team of process operators in a company making small assemblies, nine months before. She thought she had been doing well, but was rather disappointed in the annual merit pay rise she had received. Hannah asked to see her manager and said to him: 'When I took over this team, morale was low, things were badly organized and most of the people on the team were not properly trained for the jobs they were doing.'

Hannah then went on to give an account of all the work she had done to improve things since she had taken over the running of the team. Hannah's manager heard her out patiently, and then said:

'It's true that you have done very well, Hannah, and I agree with what you say. However, the fact remains that the output and quality of your team's work is still below the others. We want people to be happy and trained and well motivated. All these things are important. But you musn't forget that your team has been set up in order to help us manufacture high quality goods at an economic rate.'

_____

From what you've read of the case, do you think Hannah's manager is justified in criticizing her in this way? Jot down your views.

_____

_____

_____

Without knowing any more about the details, I think I'd broadly agree with the points made by Hannah's manager. Achievement of the main task is the team leader's prime responsibility, because **the allotted task is the reason for the workteam's existence: all other considerations are secondary**.

Management will look to the team leader to ensure that the team's task is accomplished. And the team will look to the team leader to guide them through the difficulties of achieving the task.

Achievement of the task is the team leader's main responsibility.

Of course, there are other responsibilities, as we've already hinted. Not least among these is a **responsibility towards individuals**.

3 Responsibility 2: the individual

What does 'responsibility towards individuals' mean, do you think?

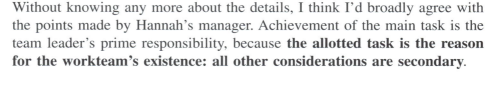

Activity 10

Read the following account, and jot down any points which it suggests to you about the responsibilities of the team leader towards the individuals in a team.

■ John Spicer was a social worker, employed by a local authority. When John's new team leader, Mary Harrison, was appointed, John was glad of the opportunity to have a long chat with her. Mary had encouraged John to speak freely about his problems. Here's an extract of what John had to say:

'Before you came, Mary, we were left very much to our own devices. We got very little support and not much encouragement. As you know, this job can be very tough at times. I've been physically attacked on a couple of occasions, for instance, by the very people I was trying to help. Also, I know people in the team who have been given jobs which they had no training or preparation for. What's more, there isn't any proper system of reviewing objectives or performance, so we don't know how well we've been doing or what is expected of us.'

You may have noticed that John made several points which remind us about the responsibility of team leaders towards individuals. These include:

- **supporting and encouraging the individual;**
- **assigning tasks appropriate to the member's abilities;**
- **making clear the job roles of the team members;**
- **assessing performance;**
- (if necessary) **protecting the individual** from other people, including other members of the group.

These are important points, so let's go through each one in turn.

3.1 Supporting and encouraging the individual

One of the best parts of belonging to a team is that you aren't on your own. In the best teams, each member can look to the others for assistance and encouragement. In particular, the team leader is ready and able to provide help, guidance and support.

This has more to do with adopting a positive and sharing approach than with any kind of management technique. Some questions you could ask yourself are:

'Do I make myself available when team members need me?'
'Do I give recognition to individual effort and achievement?'
'Do I praise loudly and criticize quietly?'
'Do I encourage everyone to make a full contribution to the team?'

3.2 Assigning appropriate tasks

When we talk about 'assigning tasks that are appropriate to the team member's abilities', we **don't** mean:

- tasks that are too easy:

as easy tasks lead to boredom. Bored people make mistakes, and become frustrated through not being able to use their full range of skills and abilities.

- tasks that are too difficult:

for people faced with tasks they can't manage become unhappy and lose confidence.

The ideal task will stretch an individual, and give a feeling of exhilaration and triumph when success has been achieved.

Matching the tasks to be performed with the capabilities of each person may require a lot of time and thought on the part of the leader. Even though perfect matching may seldom be realized, it shouldn't stop us striving for the ideal.

There are lots of ways of matching:

- If a task is too difficult for team member A, and too easy for team member B, why not get them to work together? Next time, A may be able to manage it with less help. You will have helped A develop, and given B a training and supporting role, which can be challenging and interesting in itself.
- You may find ways of making a task more demanding by, for example, setting higher targets of quality, or reducing the permitted time for completion.
- You might discover ways of making a task less demanding by, for example, breaking it down into smaller sub-tasks.
- Gaps between the abilities of individuals and the expertise required to finish a task, may be bridged by training, either on or off the job.

3.3 Clarifying job roles

As we will discuss later, role conflict and ambiguity is a common complaint, which can result in serious problems.

'Who am I? Where do I fit in? What am I supposed to be doing? In which direction am I heading?' All these questions will be asked by the team member who isn't clear about his or her role in the team. (Unfortunately, such questions are not always asked explicitly or expressed out loud.)

Work not getting done is a common symptom of uncertainty over job roles. When a task is apparently ignored or postponed without reason, the leader may have to make plain what needs to be done, who should be doing it, and (if necessary) how, when and where it should be done.

3.4 Assessing performance

Assessment is typically a key task for a team leader. Try the next Activity, to see how well you match up at the moment.

Activity 11

12 mins

This Activity may provide the basis of appropriate evidence for your S/NVQ portfolio. If you are intending to take this course of action, it might be better to write your answers on separate sheets of paper.

Explain the steps you take, or plan to take, to ensure that:

■ you communicate the purpose of assessment to everyone involved

_____

_____

_____

_____

■ you give your team opportunities to assess their own work

_____

_____

_____

_____

■ assessment of work takes place at the best times, when it is most likely to maintain and improve effective performance

_____

_____

_____

_____

■ assessments are based on evidence that is sufficiently valid and reliable

_____

_____

_____

_____

■ assessments are carried out objectively, against criteria that are clear and agreed

_____

_____

_____

_____

Your response to this Activity will depend on your own job and organization, and also on your individual approach to leadership. There are no strict rules about these things; we all have our own style and methods.

The idea of getting the team to assess its own performance may be new to you. The purpose is to encourage each person to assess his or her own performance and the performance of the team as a whole. Suitable prompting questions are:

'Did you/we reach the task objectives?'

'If not, why not: what were the precise reasons for failure? What would you do differently next time? Are the objectives themselves unrealistic?'

'If the task was successfully accomplished, what do you think you/we learned? What can we apply to other tasks? Should we set higher targets?'

'How well did we work as a team?'

'How could we do things better?'

3.5 Protecting the individual

Individuals may need protection from other team members, from other teams, from outside interference – or perhaps from themselves!

It's easy to conjure up an image of a mother hen protecting her chicks, but this analogy is perhaps a little off the mark. People at work are adults, and shouldn't need much protection, most of the time.

However, some people and some occupations are more vulnerable to manipulation, bullying and other forms of pressure than others. In an earlier Activity, John Spicer gave an account of physical attacks on staff. Social workers, teachers, police officers and those in other professions may be subject to such abuse, and may have to depend on limited systems of security to protect them. Team leaders have to do what they can to ensure that security measures are adequate for local conditions.

Forms of protection from other kinds of pressure may include:

■ clamping down on verbal abuse;
■ breaking up exclusive cliques;
■ defending team members against outside criticism;
■ encouraging more experienced members to give help and advice to those who are finding their feet.

The third responsibility of the team leader is towards **the team as a whole**.

27

4 Responsibility 3: the team

The team is made up of people and yet it also has an identity of its own.

Activity 12

Apart from the responsibilities towards individuals that we listed above, what are the leader's responsibilities towards the team as a whole?

One example is 'demonstrating a total commitment to the task and the team'. Try to list **three** other points.

_____

_____

_____

You may agree that the team leader is responsible for:

- **demonstrating a commitment** to the team;
- **setting out and agreeing the overall and specific aims and objectives**, so that everyone knows what has to be done and why it has to be done;
- **helping to ensure that the standards of the group are maintained**;
- **supporting the team when things are going against it**.

Yet another set of responsibilities concerns the relationship of the team to other groups. The team leader is also normally charged with:

- **representing the team to management**;
- **representing management to the team**;
- **co-ordinating with other teams and departments**.

This can be shown in the form of a diagram:

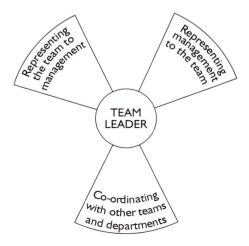

What does this mean exactly?

We can think of the leader as a hub: a central point of interest and activity. At one spoke is the team, and at a second are the other levels of organizational management. A third spoke of the wheel symbolizes other teams and people, typically including the team's direct customers and suppliers.

To say that 'the leader represents management to the team' means that:

when the team members think of the organization's management, they think first of the team leader. For, so far as they are concerned, it is the leader who is empowered to interpret higher management's demands and wishes.	if the team want to communicate with 'the powers that be', they will normally expect to do so through the leader, for he or she is their representative. (However, this does not of course mean to say that all communications must go through the leader.)

When we say 'the leader represents the team to management' we are implying that:

- the team leader's success or failure is largely dependent on the fortunes of the team;
- if higher management wish to communicate with the team, they will do so via the leader, as their representative.

In a similar fashion, the leader represents, and is a representative of, the team, in the eyes of all others, inside or outside the organization.

After all this, you may be wondering how you can cope with these various responsibilities and roles.

5 Coping with the role of team leader

5.1 Role ambiguity

If you aren't certain about some aspect of the role you are meant to be playing, you may well become confused and inefficient.

To take a simple illustration, suppose your manager tells you she is unhappy about the amount of litter in the car park and tells you to 'sort it out'.

What are you meant to do?

- Act in the role of hygienist, and get the litter picked up?
- Act in the role of disciplinarian and reprimand the people who drop litter?
- Act as liaison officer and report the matter to Security?

Of course, a situation like this would only cause you temporary uncertainty. However, if you are generally unsure of your role at work the consequences might be more damaging – to you, to the organization or both.

We can call uncertainty about roles **role ambiguity**.

As a team leader, it is largely up to you to define the job-related roles of team members and to try to ensure that role ambiguity is dealt with as far as you can.

But what about your own role?

> 'Role ambiguity results when there is some uncertainty in the minds, either of the focal person or of the members of his role set, as to precisely what his role is at any given time.'
> Charles B. Handy (1993), *Understanding Organizations* Penguin.

Activity 13

3 mins

One example of role ambiguity is being unsure about what is expected of you in terms of performance; perhaps your manager didn't make clear the standard of work required.

Have you ever been uncertain about any aspect of your role or position at work? If so, answer the following questions briefly.

What form did your own role uncertainty take?

_____

_____

_____

What did you do about it?

_____

_____

_____

You may have had an experience of, for example, uncertainty about your:

- **responsibility**

  being uncertain about just what your responsibilities were in a certain situation – say, one day when you were left in charge without specific instructions;

30

■ **expected work performance**

working for someone who wasn't consistent about the standards demanded of you or the method of assessment to be used;

■ **scope for advancement**

not knowing how you can move forward from where you are.

Situations like this are common, and should be regarded as challenges.

There is a drive among many organizations these days to devolve responsibility downwards, through continuous improvement programmes, self-managed teams, multi-skilling, empowerment and so on. If any of these changes are taking place where you work, it probably means that your role as team leader is becoming more ambiguous. You may act as spokesperson for the group but not have much in the way of authority; in this case, you are more of a **facilitator** than a leader.

Parts of the organization may operate in a non-standard way; an example is the setting up of autonomous work cells in an otherwise traditionally managed factory. You may have to report to more than one manager, or lead more than one team. Most managers are required to take on different roles from time to time. Wherever change and experimentation is going on, there is likely to be role ambiguity. So

role ambiguity is part of the experience of being a manager.

5.2 Role conflict and role incompatibility

Imagine holding a meeting of your workteam, where you are playing the role of chairperson or team leader, when your mother unexpectedly walks into the room. What is your role now?

In a situation like this, where what is expected of you in one role clashes with what is expected in another role, you can be said to be in **role conflict**.

Another condition occurs where the expectations of your role are different in different people: this is known as **role incompatibility**. For example, your team may prefer you to be the easy-going boss, while your manager expects you to be tough and uncompromising.

Role incompatibility can also occur where your **own** standards don't agree with the organization's standards, or where the image you have of yourself doesn't coincide with other people's. You could imagine a soldier who is told to shoot into a rioting mob being under great stress through role incompatibility.

31

To reduce the stress caused by role conflict or incompatibility:

■ stick to your principles of integrity and don't allow yourself to be compromised;

■ try separating your life into compartments: evenings and weekends for your social life, daytime for work life, for example;

■ be yourself – people will learn from your behaviour what to expect from you.

It isn't unknown for people to have to take on numerous roles at the same time. A familiar example is the teacher; a typical teacher has the multiple roles of: counsellor, disciplinarian, educator, caretaker, technician, adviser, accountant, child-minder . . . and so on. If you are or have been a teacher, you may care to complete the list yourself! Having too many roles can lead to role overload, which is really an exaggerated form of role conflict. Many team leaders suffer from this condition.

Activity 14

You may feel that you have too many roles to play in your job. What can anyone suffering from role overload do about it? Try to suggest **two** things.

_____

_____

_____

_____

If you are already a team leader you are probably already coping with a number of different roles, some of which will conflict. You could:

■ decide priorities, by assigning levels of importance;

■ delegate certain roles to other people;

■ (perhaps) agree with your manager that some functions be removed from your job specification.

5.3 Role underload

The opposite of role overload is role underload. It occurs when an individual feels that he or she is capable of more roles or a bigger role.

Role underload can also be stressful, because it affects self-image. People doing jobs which they feel are below their capabilities will be dissatisfied and probably inefficient.

The organization can unwittingly make things worse by telling employees how capable they are and what great prospects they have, and then proceeding to ask them to play very junior and undemanding roles. This can have the effect of making people feel very dissatisfied.

Activity 15

3 mins

Suppose you take over a new team and you feel that some of the members are probably being underutilized. Owing to the limitations of the job, there isn't a great deal of scope for expanding roles. How might you tackle this situation?

Write down your answer briefly, after a few minutes' thought.

_____

_____

_____

_____

_____

_____

_____

You may have suggested:

■ assigning roles which match capabilities wherever possible;
■ encouraging good work and effort, without building unrealistic hopes or promising opportunities which may not be realized;
■ perhaps talking to your fellow team leaders to see whether reassigning some members to other teams would be possible and beneficial to all concerned.

You may agree that role underload is probably just as common as role overload. These are the kind of problems that are a challenge to the team leader. In the next session, we look at some more challenges, as our focus turns to the team itself.

Self-assessment 2

10 mins

1 What is the team leader's main responsibility?

2 Fill in the blanks in the following sentences then use your answers to complete the grid below. When you have filled in the grid there should be another complete word in the highlighted vertical column. Some of the letters have already been filled in on the grid to give you a clue.

The responsibilities of a team leader towards the _____ in the team are:

- to _____ and _____ the individual;
- to _____ tasks appropriate to the member's abilities;
- to _____ _____ the job roles of the team members;
- to _____ performance;
- (if necessary) to _____ the individual from other people, including other members of the group.

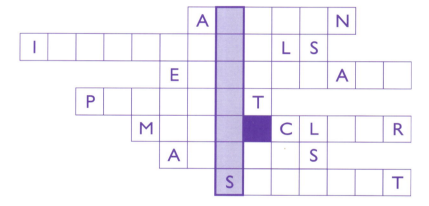

3 Identify the **incorrect** statements among the following, and explain why they are wrong:

a The team have a right to expect commitment and support from the leader, and to be able to look to the leader to clarify team roles.
b The leader is a central hub of activity and interest. All communications between management, the team, and other groups, must pass through the leader.
c Role ambiguity means that there is uncertainty about a person's role at any one time.
d Role underload means having too little to do.

Answers to these questions can be found on page 74.

6 Summary

- The leader has responsibilities to the task, the team and the individual.

- Achievement of the task is the team leader's main responsibility.

- The responsibility of team leaders towards individuals includes:
  - supporting and encouraging the individual;
  - assigning tasks appropriate to the member's abilities;
  - making clear the job roles of the team members;
  - assessing performance;
  - (if necessary) protecting the individual from other people, including other members of the group.

- So far as the team is concerned, the team leader is responsible for:
  - demonstrating a commitment to the team;
  - setting out and agreeing the overall and specific aims and objectives, so that everyone knows what has to be done and why it has to be done;
  - helping to ensure the standards of the group are maintained;
  - supporting the team when things are going against it.

- The team leader is also normally charged with:
  - representing the team to management;
  - representing management to the team;
  - co-ordinating with other teams and departments.

- Uncertainty about roles is called role ambiguity.

- When what is expected of you in one role clashes with what is expected in another role, you can be said to be in role conflict.

- When the expectations of your role are different in different people, this is known as role incompatibility.

- Role underload occurs when a individual feels that he or she is capable of more roles or a bigger role.

Session C Building and developing the team

1 Introduction

Leadership is sometimes defined as 'getting other people to do what *you* want to do because *they* want to do it'. I do not agree. If it is *your* task, why should anyone help you to achieve it? It has to be a common task, one which everyone in the group can share because they see that it has value for the organization or society and – directly or indirectly for themselves as well.

John Adair, *Effective Leadership*.[4]

John Adair's comment may remind you of Lao-Tzu: 'A leader is best when people barely know that he exists.' The task is the team's. If they have ownership of it, they are more likely to achieve it, in which case the leader can bask in their glory.

But there are always new tasks and new teams; no team stays the same for very long. Changes are taking place continually. People leave and new members join; even the leader is replaced from time to time. There is a process of continuous building and development going on.

In this session, we will trace the development of a new team. (If you are a newly-appointed leader, the team you lead is certainly 'new' in the sense that it will go through a process of upheaval, as if it was newly formed.)

EXTENSION 2
An account of the stages of team development is given in the book *Teambuilding*, by Alastair Fraser and Suzanne Neville.

Writers in this field have identified four distinct stages of team development:

forming, storming, norming and performing.

We will first look at each of these stages to see what goes on in them and to look at what actions the team leader can take to help guide the team through them.

[4] Quoted in *Effective Leadership* (Extension 1).

2 Forming

The formation of a team is a time of exploration and uncertainty. It is therefore important that the leader gives a clear lead and lays down firm targets and guidelines.

At the forming stage the team looks to the leader for standards, objectives and guidance.

2.1 Selecting the team

Activity 16

4 mins

Assuming that you have the opportunity to influence the selection of the team, what qualities would you look for in a new team member? Try to write down **two** basic criteria that are important in team selection.

_____

_____

_____

_____

_____

Probably the first consideration when selecting team members is whether they can do the job. You have to look for people with competence in the field of work.

Perhaps equally important is the ability and willingness of members to work together.

This doesn't mean that everyone must have the same kind of personality – a mix of personalities is often best. You may decide you don't want 'troublemakers': people who upset the rest of the team. Those who aren't prepared to 'pull their weight' – to contribute to the best of their abilities – may also be unwelcome in your team.

We might therefore say there are two essential qualities which any team leader would be wise to look for: the ability to do the job and the ability to fit into the team. When it comes to what might be called personal attributes, some useful questions to bear in mind are whether the potential team member:

- has a sense of humour;
- is realistic about his or her strengths and weaknesses;
- has worked successfully in a team in the past;
- appears to have integrity.

Team members should be selected on their competence, ability to fit in and personal attributes.

2.2 Setting objectives

Fundamental to running a successful workteam is knowing what your aims and objectives are, and conveying these aims and objectives to the team.

Before undertaking any task you need to know exactly what you're trying to achieve. Unless you do, your chances of accomplishing the task are small. And you certainly can't hope to lead a team into any enterprise until you have a very clear idea in your own mind of what you want done.

As a team leader or a team member, are you able to define, precisely and succinctly, the overall aim and purpose of your workteam?

Activity 17

Write down the answers to the following questions about your workteam.

- What is the overall function of your team? Put more simply, why does it exist?

For instance, if you were a supermarket supervisor you might say that the overall function of your team was to provide a check-out service for customers.

_____

_____

_____

_____

_____

■ In what special way does your team contribute to the larger aims of the organization?

The supermarket supervisor might think that team contributed to the supermarket by:

■ providing a means of collecting payments for goods, which the super-market needs to remain in existence;

■ giving the public a helpful and courteous service, which enhances the company image of 'the friendly supermarket'.

_____

_____

_____

_____

_____

■ Do all the members of your team know the answers
to the questions above? Circle your response   Yes/No

There is of course no such thing as a 'correct' response to this Activity. If you are still at all unclear about the overall objectives of your team it would be very worthwhile spending some time thinking about them.

Once the overall aims and objectives are clear and understood, they must be passed on to all members of the team. It isn't sufficient to make a statement when the group is formed, or when a new member joins. A workteam will need to be reminded about objectives periodically. This can be done in many different ways: by word of mouth; by displaying posters (for example 'Quality comes first with this team!'); perhaps best of all by example.

A workteam that is unclear about its reason for existence has little chance of succeeding.

Having decided upon overall aims and objectives, it's necessary to look at those related to individual tasks.

Ideally, all task-related objectives will be SMART.

S pecific
M easurable
A greed
R ealistic
T ime constrained

■ **Specific**

Many people 'fail' at what they're trying to do, or do not achieve what is required, simply because they aren't very sure what is expected of them. Setting non-specific targets leads to jobs being postponed for no apparent reason. People don't know what the objectives are and so tend to do something else instead.

- **Measurable**

If possible, the objectives set should be such that the outcome is capable of assessment. We looked at this topic in the previous session.

In some jobs and some industries, setting measurable objectives is easy: a production target for a team of machinists may be measurable in terms of 'garments per day', for example. In general, quantities are more easily measured than qualities, which may be more of a problem: how do you measure 'tidiness' or 'helpfulness' or 'improved layout'? The key here is in setting standards, and agreeing them with the team. For instance, you might be able to demonstrate what a tidy work area looks like, or spell out just how much trouble someone is expected to take in order to satisfy a customer.

- **Agreed**

Agreeing targets increases the incentive to reach them. Imposing work objectives without consultation may result in resentment or worse. ('What does she think we are? Robots?' 'It's all very well saying "Clear that site by midday". How do we stop people dumping more rubbish on to it?')

Again, agreeing objectives is not always feasible, especially if the objectives are set at a higher level in the company. Bear in mind that 'negotiating' targets with staff requires tact and skill. A leader who has a good rapport with his or her team will have little difficulty in agreeing what needs to be done; this won't be the case where mutual trust and confidence does not exist.

Having said this, many leaders ask the team to set their own targets. Are you bold enough to try it?

- **Realistic**

Our earlier discussion on assigning 'appropriate' tasks is relevant here. There's no point in setting unattainable targets. Asking for more than can be achieved will simply result in failure and a lowering of morale.

Generally speaking, people are at their best when they manage to rise to a challenge. Getting paid for doing less than you are capable of may make you feel that life is easy and comfortable, but there's little satisfaction in it. The best and happiest workteams are always striving to achieve something extra.

Of course, the skill is in getting the balance right. A good team leader knows what is possible and what isn't.

- **Time constrained**

Production targets are time constrained, in that they are measured by the hour, day, week or month. Most other objectives can and should be, too, because it makes more sense to require that a certain goal is accomplished within or over a specific time period.

Admittedly, open-ended objectives exist in any organization: the overall aims we discussed at the start of this section are usually, by their nature, unrestricted by time. However, it's possible and useful to introduce a time element even into continuing objectives. This is most simply done by reviewing progress and achievement at regular intervals, and asking questions such as these.

'How well were the objectives reached during the last period?'
'Do we need to improve in this or that area over the next period?'

2.3 Setting up good communication channels

At the team forming stage, the team leader must also bear in mind the necessity for good lines of communication. It is during this phase that it may be possible to tackle any problems of communication that may already exist.

Activity 18

3 mins

What barriers to good communication might exist – between team members, between the leader and the team, or between the team and the rest of the organization? Try to list **two** barriers.

_____

_____

_____

_____

_____

Answers to this Activity can be found on page 77.

A special kind of communication problem can occur when every member of the team works separately, away from the others. This situation is seen more frequently nowadays, because of the trend towards 'telecommuting' or 'home networking'. This involves people being employed from home, using modern technology to communicate with the office.

Because good communication is so vital to the effectiveness of a team, the team leader must make every effort to overcome any difficulties as soon as they arise.

2.4 Getting the team involved

At the earliest possible stage, the team leader needs to encourage team **cohesiveness** and to promote a sense of team identity and purpose. Cohesiveness describes how unified a team is; the best teams are usually highly cohesive. An important approach to achieving this unity is to get the members of the team involved in:

- planning,
- organizing,
- assessment.

We have already looked at team involvement in assessment, in Activity 11. What about the other two?

Portfolio of evidence C12.1

Activity 19

10 mins

This Activity may provide the basis of appropriate evidence for your S/NVQ portfolio. If you are intending to take this course of action, it might be better to write your answers on separate sheets of paper.

How do you currently get the team to contribute to the planning of work?

_____

_____

_____

How do you currently get the team to contribute to the organization of work?

_____

_____

_____

What more could you do to encourage involvement? List **two** or **three** ideas.

_____

_____

_____

Among the things you could do are to:

■ ask the members' opinions: show that you value their views on what is to take place;
■ seek their advice and specialized knowledge: one person can't appreciate all aspects of any matter – often members of your team will be more experienced or better informed than you are, especially in their specialist areas;
■ allow them to take part in making decisions: this increases their feelings of involvement provided the problem is not trivial or insoluble.

2.5 Encouraging team identity

Activity 20

Aside from what we've already discussed, how else would you go about encouraging team identity? What could you do, as team leader, to generate a feeling of comradeship and belonging? Try to note **two** things.

_____

_____

_____

_____

_____

_____

What you are trying to do is to encourage an attitude of mind, so that the members think of themselves as part of a team.

■ The words you use would be important here: saying 'we' and 'us' rather than 'I' and 'me'.
■ You would also want to advocate sharing of jokes, of resources, of problems, of triumphs and so on.
■ You might feel it important to create opportunities for informal social activity at work – without necessarily encroaching on members' leisure time.
■ Having a team name and 'home base' are also important to the team identity.

3 Storming

At a certain stage of team development, it is normal for conflict between team members to occur. This is the **storming** phase. The conflict mainly stems from the uncertainty felt by the members as they 'find their feet'.

It is also a period of discovery.

Activity 21

4 mins

What are the members trying to discover when they join a team? List **three** things.

_____

_____

_____

_____

_____

_____

_____

_____

Individuals are trying to discover, among other things:

- their place in the team;
- their relationships with other members ;
- the ways in which they will be expected to behave;
- the scale and complexity of the task;
- the information and resources they will need to cope;
- the best approach to the task;
- their relationship with the leader.

3.1 How the conflict may show itself

Activity 22

3
mins

How is this conflict likely to show itself, do you think? Jot down your ideas, briefly.

_____

_____

_____

The conflict may be open and obvious: disagreement and argument among the members, which in extreme cases may lead to personal hostility and aggression. There may well be a division into two or more 'sides', each representing certain opinions.

The conflict also takes place within the minds of individuals and the symptoms may therefore not be so obvious:

■ nervousness;
■ a reluctance to get down to the job;
■ sullenness;
■ spending excessive amounts of time on trivial tasks;
■ not taking part in group discussions.

These may all be signs of a lack of an individual's ability to get to grips with the real issues.

3.2 How to cope

Activity 23

3
mins

How can you, the leader, best cope with the storming stage? Write down **two** or **three** ideas for dealing with it.

_____

_____

_____

In order to deal with the uncertainty and conflict of the storming stage, you may need to:

- set an example by showing that you have confidence, clear ideas and are determined for the team to succeed;
- clarify questions if possible;
- encourage open, democratic discussion of any issues which are divisive, not allowing bullying or 'blackmail' but bringing out all the arguments;
- summarize the arguments once discussion has taken place and, if possible, get the whole group to decide;
- emphasize the importance of the task and of working together to achieve it;
- keep conflict focused on the job, rather than on personalities;
- avoid win/lose situations;
- guide and support individuals who take time to settle down.

> A win/lose situation is one in which the only possible outcomes are winning or losing. Better to give and take, and share the rewards.

Activity 24

3 mins

What about those situations where it is hard to reach agreement?

Can you think of a situation in which you were involved where the team was divided over some issue?

How was it handled?

- Did the leader force through a decision?
- Was the problem avoided or 'smoothed over', perhaps to emerge again later?
- Was a compromise solution reached?
- Did the issue get resolved by 'give and take' – a kind of negotiated solution?
- In some other way?

_____

_____

_____

_____

_____

_____

_____

Sometimes the leader has to force a decision if a reasonable attempt to reach agreement has failed. The danger here is that there will be resentment leading to further repercussions.

Avoiding, ignoring or smoothing over seldom solves anything, because it may simply postpone the problem.

A compromise solution may be achievable but the result may not please anyone.

Ideally, everyone will collaborate to reach a solution. This can take time, but may produce a good result.

Storming is a time of conflict and exploration; it can be used to help the team discover their identity.

4 Norming

A norm can be defined as a standard of behaviour which is derived from what the members of the group perceive as being acceptable and appropriate.

The norming stage is the period where the members of a group are beginning to work and act like a team. Standards are being set, in terms of:

- the methods of approach to the task;
- social behaviour;
- the roles to be played by individual members.

This stage is reached when the members have confidence in the team and the contributions they are each to make. This confidence might show itself as:

- a willingness to listen to the opinions of others;
- a pride in the team;
- genuine cohesiveness and a readiness to share;
- mutual support;
- a readiness to get on with the job.

The main danger, as group standards are established, is that the norms might not be compatible with the aims and objectives of the organization. A team leader must be aware of this, and do everything possible to:

- **encourage** the development of **positive** norms, and to
- **discourage** the development of norms that have a **negative** effect on productivity and cohesiveness.

During norming, the right norms must be established.

4.1 Making plans for the team

Key to the achievement of the team's objectives is **planning**. Plans must:

- be consistent with objectives;
- provide for all personnel in the team, taking account of the abilities and development needs of each individual;
- be realistic and achievable within the constraints imposed on and by the organization;
- be conveyed to the team in sufficient detail, and at a level and pace that individual members can cope with;
- be updated at regular intervals, because plans have to meet changing needs, and unforeseen circumstances.

Do you bear all these aspects in mind when you do your team planning?

Portfolio of evidence C12.1	Activity 25	10 mins

This Activity may provide the basis of appropriate evidence for your S/NVQ portfolio. If you are intending to take this course of action, it might be better to write your answers on separate sheets of paper.

Summarize briefly a plan that you have made recently, or are in the process of making, regarding the work of your team. This might be related to work schedules, project management, allocating work to individuals, or some other aspect of the work.

_____

_____

_____

_____

_____

_____

_____

Explain how you ensure, or intend to ensure, that your plan:

a is consistent with the objectives you have agreed with the team?

_____

_____

_____

_____

_____

b includes provision for everyone in your team, while taking into account each person's abilities and development needs?

_____

_____

_____

_____

_____

c is realistic and achievable within the constraints you have to work under?

_____

_____

_____

_____

_____

d is conveyed to your team in sufficient detail, and at a level and pace that your team members can cope with?

_____

_____

_____

_____

_____

e is updated at regular intervals?

_____

_____

_____

_____

_____

Your response to this Activity will depend upon your own approach and your work situation.

a   Matching plans with objectives might entail making sure they are both written down clearly, and perhaps getting the team's (or your manager's) agreement that the two are compatible.

b   It's easy sometimes to set out plans which ignore the needs or abilities of some of the group. For example, you may decide to assign work that is too difficult, or too easy, for a particular person. One way to check is to write everyone's name and ask yourself: 'What effects will my plan have on this individual?'

c   The team may be able to help you decide the feasibility of your plan.

d   If you know your team well, you may be confident that your plan will be understood by everyone, and that each member will be able to cope. For new teams or team members, there may be a need to monitor the members' reactions, and to ask them to confirm that nothing stands in the way of their making progress.

e   Somewhere built into your plan, there should be provision for updating it.

5   Performing

The performing phase, as the name suggests, is the time when the team begins to produce useful work. The conflict is over, the members have settled into their roles and the constructive work on the task commences.

Activity 26

2 mins

Having steered the team through the difficult earlier stages, what more is there for the leader to do? Select one phrase from the list below.

- ■   Sit back and reap the rewards. ☐

- ■   Give encouragement, but largely let the team get on with it. ☐

- ■   Work just as hard as before. ☐

There is only one answer here: having got the team over the forming, storming and norming stages, the team leader must work just as hard as before at:

- monitoring the output and quality of the work, to ensure it meets targets;
- ensuring performance is maintained;
- seeking new challenges and targets, so that performance can be improved.

A team that is not developing is stagnating.

Good teams are always striving to reach their peak. This can be observed in the very best sports teams. Other sides have a good season and get overconfident: the manager relaxes, the players look for rewards, perhaps the team even starts breaking up. The best teams win consistently, because they are never quite satisfied with their performance.

Winning next time is more important than winning last time.

The team leader's role is to:

- draw out the best from the team members;
- set ambitious but achievable targets;
- encourage effort and discourage complacency.

Most of all, the leader must lead by example – setting and maintaining high personal standards. That's what leadership is mostly about.

6 Providing feedback

- The Bramley Machinery Company made fail-safe devices for electrical equipment. One day last year they were awarded a large contract by a South American government for the supply of some of their devices, which were to be installed in very difficult environmental conditions, to safeguard electrical power equipment. This was only a small part of a huge project.

Ken Waterson, Bramley's Sales Manager, travelled several times to South America to demonstrate the equipment and eventually to sign the contract. While he was there he was given brochures which described the government project and the part it would play in building up the prosperity of the country.

On returning to England, Ken showed the brochures to the company directors. The board decided that they would ask Ken and his staff to put on a special presentation for all the company workforce, showing what the project was all about, and the small but vital contribution to it being made by the Bramley equipment.

Activity 27

3 mins

Do you think that this kind of information is useful to staff members whose job has nothing to do with selling or contracts? What effect do you think this had on the people who were working on the equipment concerned? Jot down your views briefly.

_____

_____

_____

_____

_____

_____

_____

Many would agree that this kind of background information, although it seems to have little to do with engineering, manufacturing or many of the other activities in a company, will actually be very helpful. Knowing something about how your work affects other people, other companies and other countries can be a very positive motivating factor.

People like to know:

'What effect is my work – and my team's work – having on other people?'
'Where does it fit in with the rest of the organization?'
'What happens to the goods we produce – who uses them?'
'Is the user (or the customer) happy with the work our team does?'
'What does the rest of the organization we work for get up to?'
'Are our team objectives being met?'

This was an example of feedback on an organization-wide basis, but the same need exists within every team. In particular, they need **feedback on their own work performance**. They want feedback that:

■ acknowledges achievement;
■ criticizes performance in a positive, constructive fashion;
■ gives them information that they can use to improve future performance;
■ encourages them to strive for better things.

As team leader, it's part of your job to ensure that feedback reaches the team.

Portfolio of evidence C12.3

Activity 28

15 mins

This Activity may provide the basis of appropriate evidence for your S/NVQ portfolio. If you are intending to take this course of action, it might be better to write your answers on separate sheets of paper.

a Give **three** examples of feedback that you have provided to your team in the recent past, which acknowledged achievement, and provided constructive suggestions and encouragement for improving work.

_____

_____

_____

_____

_____

_____

_____

b Explain how you ensure that feedback to your team is given at a time and place, and in a form and manner, most likely to maintain and improve performance.

_____

_____

_____

_____

_____

_____

_____

c Explain how you ensure that the feedback you give is clearly understood, and is based on an objective assessment of the team members' work.

_____

_____

_____

_____

_____

_____

_____

d What do you do to see that team members are given every opportunity to respond to feedback, and to recommend how their work could be improved?

_____

_____

_____

_____

_____

_____

_____

e How does your feedback take due account of personal circumstances and organizational constraints?

_____

_____

_____

_____

_____

_____

_____

f Explain what you do to ensure that feedback given shows respect for individuals and the need for confidentiality?

_____

_____

_____

_____

_____

_____

_____

Some possible responses to this Activity are:

a 'A team member worked particularly hard at keeping her temper when a customer was rude and abusive. I let her know that her efforts were appreciated, and that I understood how difficult it is for sales staff at times to keep in mind the slogan "the customer is always right". At the same time, I pointed out that she could call on my help or that of colleagues in tricky situations. What customers often want is to feel they are getting attention.'

b 'We hold regular team meetings, during which I will comment on progress, as I see it. At the same time, I make a point of listening to their feedback to me – it's a two-way communication. Then I make sure I talk to each member individually, and give positive guidance, encouragement and help where I can.'

c   'To ensure that feedback is understood, I don't just talk – I listen, and encourage the team member to talk to me. I try not to move on till I'm sure that we have understood one another. So far as being objective is concerned, I will try to get "a second opinion" from time to time, especially on important matters. Senior team members, or my manager are co-opted to perform this role.'

d   'This is achieved through team and individual meetings – see (b) and (c) above.'

e   'The pressures in this job can be quite high. On Saturdays, especially, the shop is usually full, and temporary, inexperienced staff are sometimes left on their own to cope. It is easy to make a fuss about one mistake, but I aim to bear in mind the fact that we all do things wrong from time to time. What I emphasize to the team is that we all have to learn from our mistakes. Everyone has "off days", and I try to make due allowance for this fact. Also, although it's the aim of the organization to make sure staff are trained, there are times when I have to use untrained people. I give them as much help as I can, and avoid too much "negative" feedback.'

f   'Respect works two ways: I can't demand respect if I don't give it. Mutual trust is important, too, and if something is said in confidence, on either side, that must also be treated with respect.'

Of course, these are just examples of the kind of answers that you might put forward. But don't forget, if you are submitting them as part of your portfolio, you will need *evidence* – perhaps in the form of witness testimony, meeting agendas, minutes and so on.

7   Co-ordinating with other teams

No team works in isolation. Even a team of Arctic explorers must maintain good contact and good relations with its supporting services.

A workteam cannot afford to become detached or aloof from the rest of the organization. That's why it is so important for the team leader to encourage a spirit of co-operation.

Activity 29

3 mins

Can you think of a way in which a workteam might become isolated?

_____

_____

_____

It is natural for a workteam to want **some** independence and not to have to rely too much on others. This could in some cases be taken too far and lead to a kind of self-sufficiency: 'We don't need anyone to help us – we can manage on our own.'

A team that is very cohesive – whose members are very close-knit – may put up barriers to 'outsiders'.

As we have discussed, poor communications may also cause difficulties in maintaining good working relationships between different parts of the same organization.

Activity 30

What other teams, sections, departments or key personnel are important to your team to help it achieve its targets?

_____

_____

_____

_____

What do you need from them and they from you?

_____

_____

_____

_____

Do you think that your team's relationships with these people are good enough in all cases? | YES | NO |

Do you think that your team's communications with these people are good enough in all cases? | YES | NO |

To what extent could the following strategies improve relationships and/or communications:

■ holding meetings?

_____

_____

_____

- reports from you or from them?

  _____
  _____
  _____

- sharing of information by including the other group on memos and reports?

  _____
  _____
  _____

- new or modified procedures?

  _____
  _____
  _____

- temporary lending/borrowing of people, so that each team gets to understand more about the other?

  _____
  _____
  _____

- holding presentations or 'open days' of the work you do or the work they do?

  _____
  _____
  _____

- informal get-togethers?

  _____
  _____
  _____

Whatever your answers, you may want to bear in mind that, as a leader, you owe allegiance to the organization you work for, as well as to your workteam. Don't forget that you are a member of this larger team and depend on support from your colleagues, just as they may feel they have a right to expect help from you.

58

Self-assessment 3

10 mins

Complete the following sentences with a suitable word or words, chosen from the list below.

1 At the _____ stage the team looks to the leader for _____, objectives and _____.

2 Team members should be selected on their _____, ability to fit in and personal _____.

3 _____ is a time of _____ and exploration; it can be used to help the team _____ their identity.

4 A workteam that is _____ about its reason for existence has little chance of succeeding.

5 During _____, the right norms must be _____.

6 _____ next time is more important than _____ last time.

ATTRIBUTES	FORMING	STORMING
COMPETENCE	GUIDANCE	UNCLEAR
CONFLICT	NORMING	WINNING
DISCOVER	STANDARDS	WINNING
ESTABLISHED		

7 Identify which of the following statements are **correct** and explain why you disagree with the others.

    a In selecting a new team, it's best to get people with the same kind of personalities and the same levels of competence.

    b During the storming stage, members are trying to discover their role in the team.

    c In resolving serious disagreement, the leader's job is to smooth things over, so that the problem is forgotten about.

    d During the performing stage, the leader's job is to monitor output and make sure standards are maintained and improved.

8 Select the ONE **incorrect** statement from the list below, and explain why it is wrong:

In dealing with the storming stage, the leader should:

    a emphasize the common task;

    b get to the heart of the personality differences;

    c encourage discussion, giving everyone a chance to speak;

    d show confidence in the team.

Answers to these questions can be found on page 74.

9 Summary

- The forming stage of team development is one of exploration and uncertainty. A clear lead and firm targets are needed.

- Team members should be selected on their competence to do the job, their ability to fit in and their personal attributes.

- A workteam that is unclear about its reason for existence has little chance of succeeding.

- Ideally, all task-related objectives will be SMART.

  S pecific
  M easurable
  A greed
  R ealistic
  T ime constrained

- An important approach to the task of increasing team cohesiveness and sense of identity is to get members involved in planning, organizing and evaluating.

- During the storming stage of team development, the members are in conflict with one another. In order to cope with the uncertainty and conflict of the storming stage the leader should show confidence, give a clear lead and emphasize the importance of the team's task.

- The norming stage is the period when the members of the group are beginning to work and act like a team. During norming, the right norms must be established.

- The performing stage is the time when the team begins to produce useful work. For the leader the emphasis changes to monitoring, maintenance and promoting higher standards.

- All teams need feedback that:

  - acknowledges achievement;
  - criticizes performance in a positive, constructive fashion;
  - gives them information that they can use to improve future performance;
  - encourages them to strive for better things.

- Co-ordination and co-operation with other groups in the organization are essential. The team leader has to make sure that good relationships and good communications are established and maintained.

Performance checks

1 Quick quiz

Jot down the answers to the following questions on *Leading Your Team*.

Question 1 'In work organizations, managers are team leaders, and team leaders are managers.' Say to what extent you agree with this statement, and briefly explain why.

_____

_____

_____

_____

Question 2 List **three** 'personal qualities' that are looked for in a team leader.

_____

_____

_____

Question 3 We listed the steps of decision making as: 1 Defining the problem; 2 Collecting information; 3 Generating alternatives; 4 Choosing the best option; 5 Implementing your choice; 6 Evaluating the result. Typically, which steps do inconsistent decision makers tend to spend too little time on?

_____

_____

_____

Question 4 'The best leaders never ask their team members to do something they couldn't do themselves.' Is this statement true, do you think? Briefly explain your answer.

_____

_____

_____

Question 5   Our three-circle model listed the three main responsibilities of the leader. What were they?

_____

_____

_____

Question 6   List **three** responsibilities that the team leader has towards the individual.

_____

_____

_____

Question 7   Now list **three** responsibilities that the team leader has towards the team as a group.

_____

_____

_____

Question 8   What kinds of prompting questions would help the team to assess its own performance?

_____

_____

_____

Question 9   Explain what you think is meant by: 'the leader represents management to the team'.

_____

_____

_____

Question 10   Match each term on the left with the correct description on the right:

a Role ambiguity.	w A clash between what is expected of you in one role and what is expected in another role.
b Role underload.	x When different people have different expectations about someone's role.
c Role incompatibility.	y Uncertainty about roles.
d Role conflict.	z When an individual feels that he or she is capable of more roles or a bigger role.

Question 11   What are the **four** recognized stages of team development, and in which order do they appear?

_____

_____

_____

_____

Question 12   What **three** main criteria would you recommend a team leader use to select new members?

_____

_____

_____

_____

Question 13   Ideally, all task-related objectives will be SMART – **S**pecific . . . and what else? What do the other letters stand for?

_____

_____

_____

_____

Question 14   During the storming stage of team development, the members are in conflict with each other. What general approach is appropriate for the team leader at this time?

_____

_____

_____

Question 15   All teams need feedback. What kind of feedback?

_____

_____

_____

Answers to these questions can be found on page 78.

2 Workbook assessment

60 mins

■   Desmond Jalland took over as team leader of a training workshop that taught the skills of the construction industry to unemployed people. He was promoted because he was good at his job and popular with the students. The workshop had limited resources, which meant that there were a lot of administrative duties that had to be undertaken by the instructors in addition to their teaching and demonstrating roles. Although five other instructors worked for him, Desmond felt obliged to take on all these extra tasks, as well as listening to students' problems, helping them to find jobs and so on. Far from helping him, the other instructors became rather critical of Desmond because he never seemed to have time for them and their needs. One instructor left, which gave Desmond a new problem of trying to find a replacement. The overall picture is one of a harassed, overworked team leader, demanding students and rather disaffected staff.

Answer the following questions. You do not need to write more than three or four sentences for each answer.

1   When Desmond took on the job of team leader, his boss told him he needn't change his way of working very much, because the workshop couldn't afford to have a team leader who wasn't also an instructor. Explain how this advice would have made Desmond's working life more difficult.

2   Describe a different approach to the job that Desmond might take – assuming that he still has to carry out his instructing duties.

3 Is he suffering from role overload or just overwork? Give a reason for your answer.

4 Which leadership skills, discussed in the workbook, do you think that Desmond needs to learn more about?

5 Which management skills does Desmond need to learn more about?

6 If you were Desmond, how would you set about making a personal plan for assessing and developing your team-leading skills, for the longer term?

Portfolio of evidence C1.1

3 Work-based assignment

60 mins

Activity 8 on page 17 is relevant to this assignment.

The time guide for this assignment gives you an approximate idea of how long it is likely to take you to write up your findings. You will find you need to spend some additional time gathering information, perhaps talking to colleagues and thinking about the assignment.

Your written response to this Assignment may provide the basis of appropriate evidence for your S/NVQ portfolio.

What you have to do

For this Assignment, your aim is to find ways of improving the effectiveness of yourself as a team leader.

1 You will need to conduct an analysis of your performance. It is very difficult to do this without help, so you will need to consult others, such as your manager, members of your team, and perhaps other friendly colleagues. Tell them you are looking for honest and constructive criticism, in assessing your skills and performance. Fairly obviously, you should only ask those whom you feel would give helpful answers.

The following list of questions is fairly comprehensive. One approach is to set them out on sheets of paper, and ask each person to give you a mark out of 10. (You may prefer them to do this anonymously, so they won't be inhibited through fear of hurting your feelings.) You can then add up the scores for each item, and average the scores. Thus you might get scores of 8, 7, 5 and 10 for 'planning', giving a total of 30 and an average of 7.5.

2 Once you have collected and analysed your responses, you are in a good position to identify your strengths and weaknesses, and to improve your performance. In order to eliminate your weak spots, you could, for example:

- request specific training;
- find a mentor to help you;
- simply decide to change your attitude and approach.

65

One thing you may want to give some thought to is whether you should be acting less as a traditional-style manager, giving instructions and controlling the work, and more as a facilitator, empowering the team to make its own decisions.

Questions you will need to consider are:

- How good are my management skills, i.e.,
  - planning
  - organizing and co-ordinating
  - monitoring and controlling
  - communicating
  - supporting and motivating
  - evaluating?
- How good am I at showing:
  - determination
  - consistency
  - dependability
  - integrity
  - fairness
  - confidence in the team?
- How good am I at:
  - giving credit where it's due
  - standing by the team when it's in trouble
  - keeping the team informed
  - supporting and encouraging the individual
  - assigning tasks appropriate to the members' abilities
  - making clear the job roles of the team members
  - assessing performance
  - protecting the individual from other people
  - demonstrating a commitment to the team
  - making clear the roles of the team members, so that everyone knows what is expected of them
  - setting out and agreeing the overall and specific aims and objectives, so that everyone knows what has to be done and why
  - helping to ensure that the standards of the group are maintained
  - supporting the team when things are going against it
  - representing the team to management
  - representing management to the team
  - co-ordinating with other teams and departments.

What you should write

You should submit:

- the results of your 'survey';
- a brief commentary on it, e.g. what surprised you about it? what do you disagree with?
- an explanation of the actions you intend to take as a result of the above, for improving your performance.

You should not need to write more than two or three pages in total. The most important purpose of your report is to convince the reader that you have a well-thought out plan for improvement.

Reflect and review

Now that you have completed your work on *Leading Your Team*, let us review our workbook objectives.

When you have completed this workbook you will be better able to assess your own leadership qualities and potential.

Throughout this workbook, we have attempted to answer questions such as: 'What is a leader?'; 'What does a leader have to be?'; 'What does a leader have to do?' As we have discussed, physical attributes – physical strength, sex, age, etc. – do not seem to be very relevant. As was mentioned in Session A, a leader has to have followers, and to get people to follow you, it's necessary to persuade and influence them: to guide their actions and opinions. This can be done in very many ways, and it is important that each would-be leader should behave in a natural manner, rather than try to copy someone else's style.

Now that you have completed your reading, and responded to the Activities, you will perhaps have a better understanding of what leadership is, and is not. If so, you should be in a better position to evaluate your own leadership qualities and potential.

Try the following questions.

■ Do you have the determination and confidence to be an excellent leader? Explain your answer, briefly.

_____

_____

_____

_____

■ How would you describe your potential as a leader?

_____

_____

_____

_____

67

The second objective was:

When you have completed this workbook you will be better able to enhance your leadership skills.

After assessment come the plans for improvement. As we discussed, most leadership skills and attributes can be learned or acquired, with the possible exception of the most basic ones of determination, a willingness to be a leader, and an enjoyment of working with people. One conclusion that was not quite expressed in so many words in the workbook was that 'almost anyone can be a leader'. Nevertheless, this is probably true. We also noted that leadership was not management, i.e. the functions of leadership and management are not the same. Nevertheless, there is a good deal of overlap between them.

Like many callings, improvement at leadership comes with practice, **provided that** you have a good understanding of what you're aiming at, and some knowledge of the necessary techniques. One excellent approach is to find a role model – someone whose leadership skills and qualities you admire. If that role model can also act as a trusted advisor, so much the better.

■ Which elements of the techniques or advice discussed are particularly relevant and useful to you, in your aspirations to become a more effective leader?

_____

_____

_____

_____

■ What have you learned that will help you better understand your aims as a leader?

_____

_____

_____

_____

The third objective of the workbook was:

When you have completed this workbook you will be better able to recognize the responsibilities of leadership, and the roles to be played by a team leader.

For convenience, we used John Adair's three-circle model to identify the triple sets of responsibility: the task, the individual and the group. The task always takes priority, because it is the whole purpose of the team. Among the responsibilities towards the individual team member, we noted: supporting and encouraging the individual; assigning tasks appropriate to the member's abilities; making clear the job roles of the team members; assessing performance; (if necessary) protecting the individual from other people, including other members of the group.

Included in the leader's responsibilities towards the team as a group were: demonstrating a commitment to the team; setting out and agreeing the overall and specific aims and objectives; helping to ensure the standards of the group are maintained; and supporting the team when things are going against it.

The team leader also: represents the team to management; represents management to the team; and co-ordinates with other teams and departments.

The leader may have many roles, which can result in role ambiguity or role conflict; to some extent, this is only to be expected.

■ If you think you have now identified most of the responsibilities you have towards your task, your team and the individuals in it, which of these responsibilities did you previously not recognize?

_____

_____

_____

_____

■ Which roles do you play as team leader?

_____

_____

_____

_____

The last workbook objective was:

When you have completed this workbook you will be better able to find ways of developing your team so that it becomes more efficient and effective.

We have reviewed the stages of team development – forming, storming, norming and performing – and you have read about the kinds of activities that tend to occur at each stage. We also looked at some of the actions which the team leader may need to take, to keep the team on track towards unity and high performance.

At the forming stage, leadership actions may include: setting objectives; establishing good communication channels; getting the team involved; and encouraging team identity. During the storming stage, when there is conflict originating from uncertainty, the leader has to: set an example; clarify questions; encourage open, democratic discussion; summarize the arguments; emphasize the importance of the task; keep conflict focused on the job; avoid

69

win/lose situations; guide and support individuals who take time to settle down.

During norming, the collection of individuals is beginning to act as a unit. The leader must be aware of this, and do everything possible to encourage the development of positive norms and discourage undesirable ones.

Once performing, the team leader's role consists of: finding ways to get the best from team members; setting appropriate targets; encouraging effort; and discouraging complacency.

Some final questions to consider are:

■ What stage has your team reached? What stage should it have reached? What, if anything, is going wrong?

_____

_____

_____

_____

■ From what you have read, and looking back on your experiences, what will you do differently in future, to develop your team on the right lines?

_____

_____

_____

_____

2 Action plan

Use this plan to further develop for yourself a course of action you want to take. Make a note in the left-hand column of the issues or problems you want to tackle, and then decide what you intend to do, and make a note in Column 2.

The resources you need might include time, materials, information or money. You may need to negotiate for some of them, but they could be something easily acquired, like half an hour of somebody's time, or a chapter of a book. Put whatever you need in Column 3. No plan means anything without a timescale, so put a realistic target completion date in Column 4.

Finally, describe the outcome you want to achieve as a result of this plan, whether it is for your own benefit or advancement, or a more efficient way of doing things.

Desired outcomes		1 Issues	2 Action	3 Resources	4 Target completion		Actual outcomes

3 Extensions

Extension 1

Book   *Effective Leadership*
Author   John Adair
Edition   1983
Publisher Gower

This book covers all aspects of leadership. It is stimulating and lively, and is not difficult to read. There are three parts: Understanding Leadership; Developing your Leadership Abilities; Growing as a Leader.

Extension 2

Book   *Teambuilding*
Authors Alastair Fraser and Suzanne Neville
Edition   1993
Publisher The Industrial Society

A light and easy read, this book covers the main topics of teambuilding. To quote from its introduction: 'This publication is not designed to be a "quick fix" and it certainly won't change your life in 10 minutes, but our purpose is to identify and understand the issues and actions of successful teambuilding.'

Extension 3

Book   *Organizational Behaviour*
Authors Andrzej Huczynski and David Buchanan
Edition   Second edition 1991
Publisher Prentice Hall

This book is written from two points of view: management and the social sciences. It is divided into five parts: The individual in the organization; Groups in the organization; Technology in the organization; Structural influences on behaviour; Management in the organization. The most relevant chapters to our subject are: Chapter 15 – Organizational structure and Chapter 19 – Leadership and management style.

These Extensions can be taken up via your NEBS Management Centre. They will either have them or will arrange that you have access to them. However, it may be more convenient to check out the materials with your personnel or training people at work – they may well give you access. There are other good reasons for approaching your own people; for example, they will become aware of your interest and you can involve them in your development.

4 Answers to self-assessment questions

Self-assessment 1 on page 18

1 To be a leader, you need DETERMINATION to succeed, and to like working with PEOPLE.

2 People tend to be DEPENDABLE when others EXPECT them to be.

3 To get the RESPECT of a team, you need to be honest with them, and show you care about certain IDEALS.

4 Few of us are always FAIR. All that others can expect of you is that you try very hard to be fair.

5 To be CONSISTENT in your decision-making, be clear in your mind about the problem, and then collect FACTS and OPINIONS before you decide.

6 To LEAD others, it helps to be EXPERIENCED in the work they do.

7 The way that a leader's BEHAVIOUR is viewed by others will largely determine how SUCCESSFUL the leader is.

8 The complete diagram is:

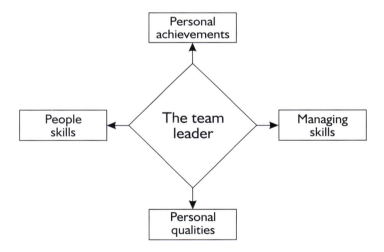

9 The six characteristics recognized as being important in good leadership are:

dependability
ability to listen
good communication skills
integrity
ability to inspire confidence
good managing skills

Self-assessment 2 on page 34

1   The team leader's main responsibility is to the task.

2   The responsibilities of a team leader towards INDIVIDUALS are to:

- SUPPORT and ENCOURAGE the individual;
- ASSIGN tasks appropriate to the member's abilities;
- MAKE CLEAR the job roles of the team members;
- ASSESS performance;
- (if necessary) PROTECT the individual from other people, including other members of the group.

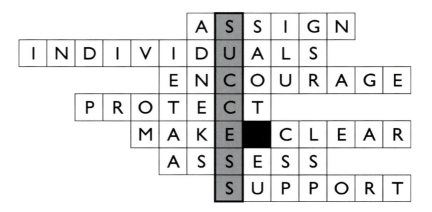

3   The **incorrect** statements are:

b   The leader is a central hub of activity and interest. All communications between management, the team, and other groups must pass through the leader. (This is not correct, because the team leader does not usually handle all communications 'in and out' of the team, even though he or she is often at the hub of communications.)

d   Role underload means having too little to do. (Role underload means having too few roles, which is not the same thing.)

Self-assessment 3 on page 59

1   At the FORMING stage the team looks to the leader for STANDARDS, objectives and GUIDANCE.

2   Team members should be selected on their COMPETENCE, ability to fit in and personal ATTRIBUTES.

3   STORMING is a time of CONFLICT and exploration; it can be used to help the team DISCOVER their identity.

4   A workteam that is UNCLEAR about its reason for existence has little chance of succeeding.

5   During NORMING, the right norms must be ESTABLISHED.

6   WINNING next time is more important than WINNING last time.

7   The **correct** statements are:

b   During the storming stage, members are trying to discover their role in the team.

d   During the performing stage, the leader's job is to monitor output and make sure standards are maintained and improved.

The **incorrect** ones are:

a   *In selecting a new team, it's best to get people with the same kind of personalities and the same levels of competence.* This is wrong because there are a range of roles to be filled in any team, and if everyone has the same kind of personality it's likely that a number of roles will not be taken up.

c   *In resolving serious disagreement, the leader's job is to smooth things over, so that the problem is forgotten about.* Where there's serious disagreement, 'smoothing things over' will not eradicate the root cause, and so the problem won't go away.

8   The one **incorrect** statement is:

In dealing with the storming stage, the leader should:

b   get to the heart of the personality differences. (This is wrong because the conflict should be kept impersonal: bringing personalities into it will not help.)

5 Answers to activities

**Activity 4
on page 9**

Check your answers against the following.

Categorize the leadership qualities we have listed into the four groups, and then say which of them you think can be learned or acquired.

	People skills	Personal qualities	Managing skills	Personal achievements	Can be learned
The ability to inspire confidence	☑	☑	☐	☐	☑
Determination	☐	☑	☐	☐	?
Dependability	☐	☑	☐	☐	☑
Integrity	☐	☑	☐	☐	☑
A history of success and achievement	☐	☐	☐	☑	☑
Fairness	☐	☑	☐	☐	☑
Listening skills	☑	☐	☑	☐	☑
Consistency	☐	☑	☐	☐	☑
A genuine interest in others	☐	☑	☐	☐	?
Displaying confidence in the team	☑	☐	☐	☐	☑
Giving credit where it's due	☑	☐	☐	☐	☑
The willingness to stand by the team	☑	☐	☐	☐	☑
Being good at keeping the team informed	☑	☐	☑	☐	☑

Those ticked in more than one of the first four columns are:

■ **The ability to inspire confidence**

You might argue that this is a personal quality, because it stems from the behaviour and image of the leader; you could also claim that it is a people skill, as confidence can be gained through talking with them.

76

■ **Listening skills**

This is both a people skill and a managing skill, because it is about communication.

■ **Being good at keeping the team informed**

Another communication skill – the same reasoning applies.

**Activity 18
on page 42**

Some barriers you may have thought of are:

■ noise;
■ working in the open air;
■ having to wear helmets or ear protection;
■ physical separation between members, or an isolated team,
■ working away from the rest of the organization;
■ a team leader who sits in an office well away from the team;
■ jargon or technical language which not everyone can understand;
■ members having limited knowledge of English;
■ inability of some members to read or write;
■ members or teams who won't communicate with others.

Organizational barriers may exist, too, such as two teams never being given the opportunity to talk together, or a manager who's simply too busy to spend time discussing anything that's not urgent or important.

There may be psychological barriers: a leader who is seen as unapproachable may be an effective, if unwitting, block to communication; and peer pressure may inhibit individuals from reporting problems, if by doing so they will be labelled as 'weak'.

You may have mentioned other kinds of barrier: people not passing on messages or passing on the wrong message (whether accidentally or deliberately); people making wrong assumptions about the understanding of others ('Didn't you know? I thought everyone knew!'); lack of training in certain kinds of equipment, which might make banks of data held on a computer system (for example) inaccessible to those who don't know how to access it.

This list is by no means exhaustive.

6 Answers to the quick quiz

Answer 1   Managers are generally expected to lead teams, but the functions of management do not entirely coincide with the qualities required of leadership.

Answer 2   You could have mentioned: integrity, fairness, consistency or determination.

Answer 3   Although inconsistent decision makers may **appear** to waver between steps 4 and 5, most typically they don't spend enough time and effort on steps 1 and 2.

Answer 4   In an ideal world, all team leaders would be capable of completing all the tasks undertaken by team members. However, modern work is often very complex, and often it just isn't possible to learn to do everything. These days, teams usually include one or more specialists, and the team leader has to find ways of managing such people without necessarily understanding everything they do.

Answer 5   The three responsibilities were to the task, to the individual and to the team:

Answer 6   You might have mentioned:

- supporting and encouraging the individual;
- assigning tasks appropriate to the member's abilities;
- making clear the job roles of the team members;
- assessing performance;
- (if necessary) protecting the individual from other people, including other members of the group.

Answer 7   You could have listed any **three** of the following:

- demonstrating a commitment to the team;
- setting out and agreeing the overall and specific aims and objectives, so that everyone knows what has to be done and why;
- helping to ensure that the standards of the group are maintained;
- supporting the team when things are going against it.

Answer 8   The questions mentioned in the workbook were:

- 'Did you/we reach the task objectives?'
- 'If not, why not: what were the precise reasons for failure? What would you do differently next time? Are the objectives themselves unrealistic?'
- 'If the task was successfully accomplished, what do you think you/we learned? What can we apply to other tasks? Should we set higher targets?'
- 'How well did we work as a team?'
- 'How could we do things better?'

Answer 9   The team think of the team leader first when they think of the organization's management. So far as they are concerned, it is the leader who is empowered to interpret higher management's demands and wishes. In addition, communications from the team would normally go through the leader, as their representative.

Answer 10   The correct matches are:

a Role ambiguity.	y Uncertainty about roles.
b Role underload.	z When an individual feels that he or she is capable of more roles or a bigger role.
c Role incompatibility.	x When different people have different expectations about someone's role.
d Role conflict.	w A clash between what is expected of you in one role and what is expected in another role.

Answer 11   The stages in order are: forming, storming, norming and performing.

Answer 12   Team members should be selected on their competence to do the job, their ability to fit in and their personal attributes.

Answer 13   SMART stands for **S**pecific; **M**easurable; **A**greed; **R**ealistic; **T**ime constrained.

Answer 14   In order to cope with the uncertainty and conflict of the storming stage the leader should show confidence, give a clear lead and emphasize the importance of the team's task.

Answer 15   All teams need feedback that:

- acknowledges achievement;
- criticizes performance in a positive, constructive fashion;
- gives them information that they can use to improve future performance;
- encourages them to strive for better things.

79

7 Certificate

Completion of this certificate by an authorized person shows that you have worked through all the parts of this workbook and satisfactorily completed the assessments. The certificate provides a record of what you have done that may be used for exemptions or as evidence of prior learning against other nationally certificated qualifications.

Pergamon Open Learning and NEBS Management are always keen to refine and improve their products. One of the key sources of information to help this process are people who have just used the product. If you have any information or views, good or bad, please pass these on.

NEBS
MANAGEMENT
DEVELOPMENT

SUPER SERIES

THIRD EDITION

Leading Your Team

....

has satisfactorily completed this workbook

Name of signatory   ....

Position   ....

Signature   ....

Date   ....

Official stamp

SUPER SERIES

SUPER SERIES 3

0-7506-3362-X   Full Set of Workbooks, User Guide and Support Guide

A. Managing Activities

B. Managing Resources

C. Managing People

D. Managing Information

SUPER SERIES 3 USER GUIDE + SUPPORT GUIDE

SUPER SERIES 3 CASSETTE TITLES

To Order - phone us direct for prices and availability details
(please quote ISBNs when ordering)
College orders: 01865 314333 • Account holders: 01865 314301
Individual purchases: 01865 314627 (please have credit card details ready)

We Need Your Views

We really need your views in order to make the Super Series 3 (SS3) an even better learning tool for you. Please take time out to complete and return this questionnaire to Trudi Righton, Pergamon Flexible Learning, Linacre House, Jordan Hill, Oxford, OX2 8DP.

Name :..

Address :..

....

Title of workbook :...

If applicable, please state which qualification you are studying for. If not, please describe what study you are undertaking, and with which organisation or college:

....

Please grade the following out of 10 (10 being extremely good, 0 being extremely poor):

Content   ....   Appropriateness to your position   ....

Readability   ....   Qualification coverage   ....

What did you particularly like about this workbook?
....
....
....

Are there any features you disliked about this workbook? Please identify them.
....
....
....

Are there any errors we have missed? If so, please state page number: ....

How are you using the material? For example, as an open learning course, as a reference resource, as a training resource etc.

....

How did you hear about Super Series 3?:

Word of mouth: ☐   Through my tutor/trainer: ☐   Mailshot: ☐

Other (please give details):...

....

Many thanks for your help in returning this form.